THE MAN FROM U.N.C.L.E. COLLECTIBLES

John Buss

AMBERLEY

First published 2019

Amberley Publishing
The Hill, Stroud
Gloucestershire, GL5 4EP

www.amberley-books.com

Copyright © John Buss, 2019

The right of John Buss to be identified as the
Author of this work has been asserted in accordance
with the Copyrights, Designs and Patents Act 1988.

ISBN 978 1 4456 8858 9 (print)
ISBN 978 1 4456 8859 6 (ebook)

British Library Cataloguing in Publication Data.
A catalogue record for this book is available from
the British Library.

Typeset in 10pt on 13pt Celeste.
Typesetting by Aura Technology and Software
Services, India. Printed in the UK.

Contents

Chapter One
Open Channel 'D'

This was American television at its best, and no other 1960s spy series came any cooler than this. Produced by MGM Television and Arena Productions, *The Man from U.N.C.L.E.* (United Network Command for Law and Enforcement) was almost a direct result of the success of the James Bond movies, even though the series had in fact been in development since 1961, prior to the release of the first Bond movie, *Dr No*, in November 1962.

Norman Felton, the series creator, had originally been interested in the spy aspects of some of Alfred Hitchcock's films of the 1940s and '50s, such as *North by Northwest*, but then became attracted to Ian Fleming's works, particularly his series of essays *Thrilling Cities* rather than the James Bond novels. In fact, Ian Fleming did become involved in the early development of the series, though his final contribution was little more than the name Napoleon Solo.

Fleming would withdraw from the project, for reasons of health but also because he was reluctant to get himself drawn into legal issues similar to those he faced over the rights to *Thunderball*. Fleming did contribute one other name into the U.N.C.L.E. mix that was to eventually make it into the series. In Fleming's version of U.N.C.L.E., Solo's boss was to have had a secretary much akin to the Moneypenny character in his Bond novels. That secretary was named April Dancer, a name that was later used in the spin-off sister series *The Girl from U.N.C.L.E.*

After Fleming departed, the show became the chronicles of Napoleon Solo (Robert Vaughn) and Illya Nickovitch Kuryakin (David McCallum), U.N.C.L.E.'s favourite nephews, who each week for 105 episodes would combat the menace of THRUSH, for the most part. The threats in U.N.C.L.E. were global. Indeed, U.N.C.L.E. itself was presented as an international organisation, owing no allegiance to any one government. And it became a smash hit.

Here in the midst of the Cold War was a spy series that had an American and a Russian agent who were not opposing each other but were instead working side by side, for the larger cause of world peace. As explained in the first season's opening titles, 'U.N.C.L.E. is an organisation consisting of agents of all nationalities. It's involved in maintaining political and legal order anywhere in the world.' Early episodes also contained personal introductions from the three principles, whereby they spoke directly into the camera explaining their role in the U.N.C.L.E. organisation.

This in itself was part of U.N.C.L.E.'s success or appeal. The pretence of this fictional organisation being real brought a sense of realism to the show. Each episode even ended with a disclaimer to enhance this realism: 'We wish to thank the United Network Command for Law and Enforcement, without whose assistance this programme would not be possible.'

The series also owes much to the casting. The teaming of Vaughn and McCallum, the tongue-in-cheek humour and banter between them was just enough to give the right feel without going over the top and becoming silly. You could believe in the characters, because the actors appeared to believe in their situations.

To Trap a
Spy UK Quad
poster.

The first season of twenty-nine black and white episodes first aired in 1964, starting with 'The Vulcan Affair', which, in a slightly different and longer form, was released as the feature film *To Trap a Spy*. In all, eight U.N.C.L.E. films were produced by combining fifteen episodes along with some occasional new footage added. It is possibly thanks to these films that the series has remained as popular as it still is (in my case it was these films that first introduced me to the series). Barley a year goes by without one or another of the films being broadcast in the UK.

Only ninety of the 105 episodes were shown in the UK, as the episodes used to make the films were not sold to TV companies in countries where the films were to be on general release. Likewise, the last five U.N.C.L.E. films were not shown in the USA. American audiences were not impressed with the idea of paying to see an episode at the cinema that they were able to watch on television for free, as had been the case with the first three films. Along with the original eight films and the 105 episodes, Napoleon and Illya also returned in 1983 for a one-off TV movie entitled *The Fifteen Years Later Affair*. Enjoyable as it was, being one of the highest rated TV movies of the year, sadly no full-scale revival of the series followed the 1983 reunion.

All episodes of the original series had always ended with the word 'affair', so it was only right that this should be repeated when it returned in 1983. Other series used similar conventions. *Burkes Law,* for instance, had its own gimmick where each episode began with 'Who Killed...', while *The Wild Wild West* always started episodes with 'The Night of... '.

In more recent times, a new big-screen version of the series, directed by Guy Ritchie, was produced by the current copyright holders, Warner Brothers. Released in 2015, this new U.N.C.L.E. was an entirely different spin on the series and focused on the first meeting and pairing up of Napoleon and Illya, with the creation of the U.N.C.L.E. organisation taking place only at the end of the movie. Though proving a great critical success, the movie did not do as well as it deserved at the box office, suffering from the release of the fifth *Mission Impossible* film only a few weeks earlier. It also proved to be extremely divisive

Return of the Man from U.N.C.L.E. promotional handout.

among fans of the original series. There were those who wholeheartedly embraced this new movie and welcomed the exposure that it afforded the series, while others refused point-blankly to acknowledge it and were actively disparaging of the movie, even during its production, because it did not feature the original actors – the parts of Napoleon and Illya were played by Henry Cavill and Armie Hammer respectively. It should be noted, however, that this film's release sparked both new interest in the original series, with a whole new (albeit small) set of younger fans being introduced to the series off the back of the film, and a small increase in the demand for, and prices of, the original 1960s products.

A remarkable array of different products, with everything from bubble gum to wristwatches, was issued in connection with this series. Few other shows at the time came close to the range of products issued for U.N.C.L.E. (today this amount of spin-offs is commonplace). It must be remembered that though a larger range of products exists for *Star Trek* (with new items coming out all the time), most of this did not occur until *Star Trek*'s syndication in the early 1970s. (Interestingly, the first pairing of Shatner and Nimoy, prior to *Star Trek*, takes place in an U.N.C.L.E. first season episode, 'The Project Strigas Affair'.) There were quite possibly more U.N.C.L.E. products issued in America during the 1960s than for almost any other TV series at the time.

As the deadline approached for this guide, it became increasingly apparent that while a fair percentage of these 1960s U.N.C.L.E. products have been included, a huge swathe of items would not be able to be, purely due to space restrictions. For this reason, this guide concerns itself primarily with items of original merchandise: i.e. those products produced at the time of the series' original run, or soon after. Items that are not contemporary with the series but have been issued or published since the 1960s have been excluded.

Assembled Napoleon Solo gun.

Chapter Two
Merchandise Briefing

Even before the series had gone into production, the producers had visions of generating more than just advertising revenue. Recognising the show's potential appeal to teens and pre-teens, Arena Productions decided to engage the services of the Stanley Weston Company to maximise this appeal and potential marketing opportunities. Stanley Weston suggested to U.N.C.L.E. executive producer Norman Felton that certain

Napoleon Solo Gun set, first style box.

Napoleon Solo Gun set, third style box. (Warner Todd Huston collection)

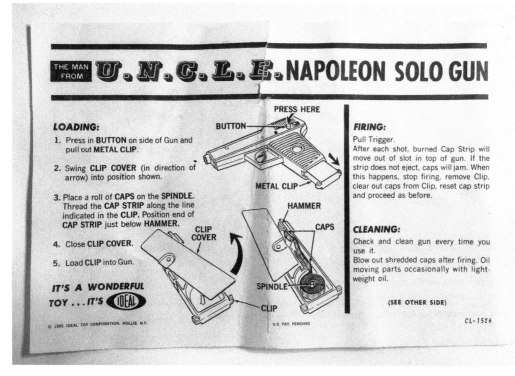

THE MAN FROM U.N.C.L.E. NAPOLEON SOLO GUN

LOADING:

1. Press in **BUTTON** on side of Gun and pull out **METAL CLIP**.

2. Swing **CLIP COVER** (in direction of arrow) into position shown.

3. Place a roll of **CAPS** on the **SPINDLE**. Thread the **CAP STRIP** along the line indicated in the **CLIP**. Position end of **CAP STRIP** just below **HAMMER**.

4. Close **CLIP COVER**.

5. Load **CLIP** into Gun.

IT'S A WONDERFUL TOY ... IT'S IDEAL

© 1965 IDEAL TOY CORPORATION, HOLLIS, N.Y.

PRESS HERE

BUTTON

METAL CLIP

HAMMER

CLIP COVER

CAPS

SPINDLE

CLIP

U.S. PAT. PENDING

FIRING:

Pull Trigger.
After each shot, burned Cap Strip will move out of slot in top of gun. If the strip does not eject, caps will jam. When this happens, stop firing, remove Clip, clear out caps from Clip, reset cap strip and proceed as before.

CLEANING:

Check and clean gun every time you use it.
Blow out shredded caps after firing. Oil moving parts occasionally with light-weight oil.

(SEE OTHER SIDE)

CL-1526

Napoleon Solo Gun set instructions. (Warner Todd Huston collection)

areas of the series should be developed with a particular eye towards merchandising. One such suggestion was that of developing what would become the U.N.C.L.E. Special Carbine Pistol. Indeed, many of the guns featured in the series did not derive from story needs, but from the suggestions of the Stanley Weston Company, with merchandising considerations chief in mind.

The original pistol used was a modified German Mauser, with various attachments. The Mauser was later exchanged for a Walther P38 pistol. Ideal Toys, the company that marketed the U.N.C.L.E. toys in the US, was not keen on the Mauser version of the gun, so with the help of Reuben Klemmer, who had worked on the original design for the series, they developed their own version. Interestingly, Lone Star Toys, who were to issue a die-cast version of the U.N.C.L.E. Special in the UK, based its version of the gun on a Mauser, though of a different style to the Mauser used in the series. Also of note is the fact that Lone Star later also produced a Walther P38-based U.N.C.L.E. Special as well.

Napoleon Solo Gun Set, Ideal Toys, 1965

This was the first of the Ideal-produced gun sets in the USA. The set contained an ID badge showing the number six (for an unexplained reason since no one on the show ever used a number six). This number appeared on all ID badges issued with the various Ideal gun sets, which included an ID card with black type on a silver-printed card and a gun with a scope, extended stock and extended barrel. A bipod was also included. This cap-firing gun was plastic with a clip container for the caps, which was somewhat of a unique feature to cap guns produced by Ideal. This gun became the standard Ideal-issue cap gun that would then appear in almost all of their U.N.C.L.E. gun sets, with the exception of the Illya Kuryakin set. There appears to be three distinct packaging phases for this product, though the difference between the first and second issues seems to be only in the quality of the printing. The first issue, printed on corrugated cardboard, had a box printed in dull blue, orange and black, with a backing card for the contents printed in dull orange. The first two versions featured an image of Napoleon taken from the board game also produced by them, attached to the box front. The second issue saw glossier printing with much brighter and more vibrant colours.

The final, third box version sees more contrast in the colours used, while the picture of Solo is now printed onto the box instead of being the removable piece it had previously been. The original issue price for the set in 1965 was $3.66, which equates to around $29 by today's pricing. This set was immensely popular and had sales in advance of $600,000 before even hitting the stores.

Napoleon Solo Gun set mail-order box. (Warner Todd Huston collection)

Along with the basic set there was also the Sears mail-in exclusive edition. This was produced in a plain cardboard box containing all of the usual items issued in the regular set along with the addition of a silver ID badge sticker and one of the small guns with a holster from the Stash-Away set that the company would also issue.

One further variation, and possibly the rarest edition of this gun, is the Canadian edition, which was issued in almost exactly the same box as the board game that Ideal also produced, but with the word 'Game' being removed from the box lid. The membership badge contained within the set was also different to the standard US-issued membership card, it being on a thicker blue card stock as opposed to the silver cards issued in the American sets. The Canadian cards are also duel printed, with English on one side and French on the other.

Napoleon Solo Gun set Canadian box contents.

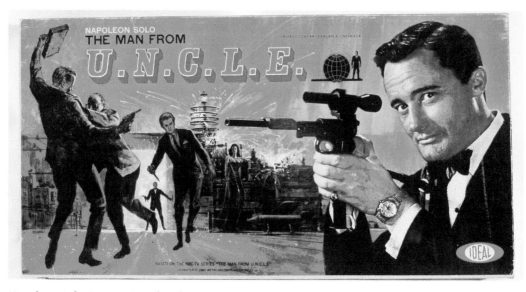

Napoleon Solo Gun set Canadian box.

Ideal Toys Canadian ID card. (Warner Todd Huston collection)

Ideal Toys Canadian ID card reverse. (Warner Todd Huston collection)

Ideal Toys American issue ID card.

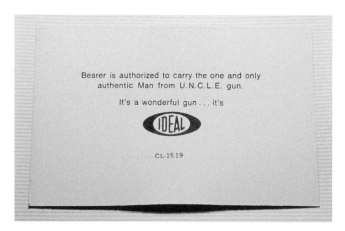

Ideal Toys American
ID card reverse.

Secret Service Gun Set, Ideal Toys, 1965

As stated above, in order to maximise sales, and no doubt save costs, the basic Ideal gun would appear in several different sets (and not only U.N.C.L.E. sets). The Secret Service gun set, also issued in 1965, was one such, containing said gun, an ID card and badge along with the addition of a holster. They all came displayed in a window box at the attractive price of $2.39.

Secret Service Gun set trade
catalogue advert.

Secret Weapon set. (Warner Todd Huston collection)

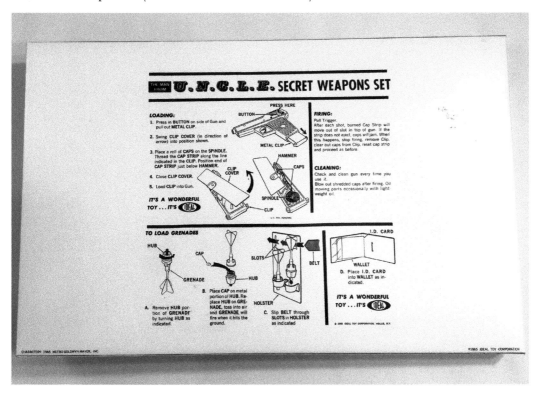

Secret Weapon set box reverse. (Warner Todd Huston collection)

Secret Weapon Set, Ideal Toys, 1965

The next of the 1965-issued sets was the Secret Weapon set, which contained all of the contents featured in the Secret Service gun set, along with the addition of two grenades in their own specially designed holster and a wallet. This also came displayed in an attractive window box.

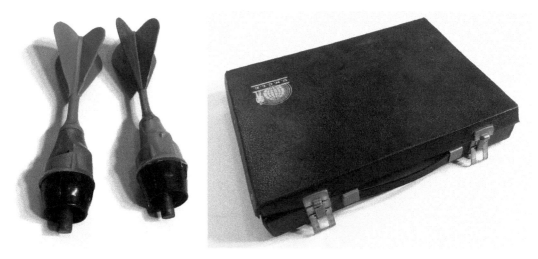

Above left: Ideal cap bombs. (Warner Todd Huston collection)

Above right and below: Ideal Attaché Case. (Warner Todd Huston collection)

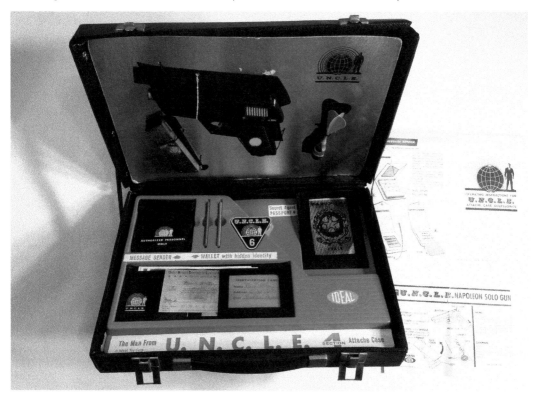

Ideal Credentials and Secret Agent Communications Set. (Warner Todd Huston collection)

Attaché Case, Ideal Toys, 1965

While this is one of the nicest looking of the U.N.C.L.E. sets produced by Ideal, this is still largely a repackaging of the same basic components: the standard gun, ID card and badge, this time being joined by a passport, secret wallet and a solitary grenade. These grenades are known to appear in two colour combinations, which appear randomly in the two sets they were used in: the Attaché Case and Secret Weapon sets. The cap bombs were produced from a fairly thin, delicate plastic with a metal plunger mechanism. They can appear with either silver fins with a blue base, or blue fins with a silver base. The reason for these variants is purely an economical one due to the positioning of components within the injection mould. Also contained within the set were two paper instruction sheets, one for the operation of the gun and the other showing the operation for all the other components. Unlike other Ideal issues, this set has very little in the way of packaging, the case itself being the main packaging. Around this was a colourful wrap-around card display label featuring images of Napoleon and Illya, as well as the set's contents. While this label just presents the set as an attaché case, the plastic tray within calls the set the 'Section 4 Attaché Case'.

Credentials and Secret Agent Communications Set, Ideal Toys, 1965

There was a crafty way of selling the same items more than once: repackaging the contents into 'new' sets. This set is little more than the base tray section from the Attaché Case presented upon a backing card with a display header. The contents included the standard No. 6 badge, message sender, wallet, passport and a couple of plastic pens. This is possibly one of the rarest of all the Ideal sets to have been issued, not so much due to its contents, but its packaging, with all of its contents being just standard-issue Ideal Toys U.N.C.L.E. pieces that could come from any number of different sets. The same holds true for the next two items, which once again offer up the same contents just repackaged. What makes them interesting is the brightly coloured header cards.

Credentials & Secret Message Sender set.

Credentials & Secret Message Sender Set, Ideal Toys, 1965

As stated before, several of the same items were recycled, and this one contained just the message sender with a pen, standard badge and ID card.

4083-2   CREDENTIALS & SECRET AGENT PASSPORT
A "must" for secret agents on the go, an official U.N.C.L.E. passport with hidden I.D. compartment in slim case, plus U.N.C.L.E. wallet with concealed I.D. card. Shrink-wrapped with colorful header.

Pack per doz: 3   **Wgt: 11 lbs.**

4084-0   CREDENTIALS & SECRET MESSAGE SENDER
This exciting coded message sender has two special pens and can reveal or conceal messages with a flick of the special colored film. Complete with U.N.C.L.E. badge and I.D. card in shrink-wrapped pack with header.

Pack per doz: 3   **Wgt: 11 lbs.**

4085-7   MAN FROM U.N.C.L.E. CREDENTIALS DEAL
Contains 18 each of: 4083-2 and 4084-0

Pack: 1 deal per carton   **Weight: 11 lbs**

Credentials & Secret Agent Passport set, Ideal trade catalogue advert.

Above left: Ideal Target Game. (Warner Todd Huston collection)

Above right: Ideal Target Game box reverse. (Warner Todd Huston collection)

Credentials & Secret Agent Passport Set, Ideal Toys, 1965
This one, sold as the Credentials & Secret Agent Passport set, contains just the toy passport, standard-issue badge and the ID card. Talk about getting your money's worth from the production costs! With both this set and the previous one, dealers were offered a special deal to bulk-buy these sets for their stores.

Target Game, Ideal Toys, 1965
Another of Ideal's initial offerings in 1965 was the Target set. This nicely presented and colourful game takes the form of a building frontage with cut-out open windows. To make

Right and overleaf:
U.N.C.L.E. Board Game by Ideal.

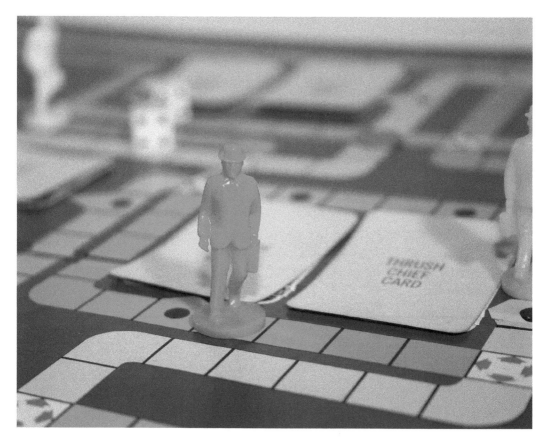

it more colourful, cut-away images show exciting drawings of what's taking place within the building. The building itself was made of thick card while the targets, which are on a swivel rod, are made of plastic. By hitting one target you would cause a different target to appear at one of the other windows. Quite a powerful toy suction dart gun came with this set, along with three suction darts.

U.N.C.L.E. Board Game, Ideal Toys, 1965

One of the best-selling Ideal Toys products of 1965, issued at a price of $2.19, was the board game. The box lid shows a photo of Napoleon Solo with an illustrated background of an exploding computer complex, and it is this image of Napoleon that was also used on the Napoleon Solo Gun set. The illustrated lid is action-packed, depicting men fighting and a tied-up young lady, with Illya running towards the fighting men and Solo standing in a doorway at the rear – all very exciting. It's a shame the gameplay doesn't live up to all this; instead, it was a rather dull and basic game, the object being for players to successfully capture a THRUSH agent that matches their assignment card, and then to return to base with the captive. This game was also issued in Canada with the addition of a French instruction sheet and a small print on the box lid advertising the fact. This same box design is also the one used for the Canadian issue of the Napoleon Solo Gun set. Showing the worldwide popularity of the series, this game was also released in Greece the following year.

THE MAN FROM U.N.C.L.E.

A GAME FOR 2 TO 4 PLAYERS

The word is out—"THRUSH is planning something big". Quickly, U.N.C.L.E. is alerted and counters by assigning men to capture the THRUSH CHIEFS. As The Man from U.N.C.L.E. you're off to capture a Chief as quickly as possible and return to headquarters to word off disaster. Enemy THRUSH Agents are everywhere waiting and watching your every move. Encounters are imminent. You must battle your way through overwhelming odds in order to complete your assignment.

OBJECT OF THE GAME

For a player to find the THRUSH Chief Card which matches his Assignment Card and return with it to U.N.C.L.E. Headquarters.

MATERIALS

Game Board, Dice, U.N.C.L.E. Assignment Cards, U.N.C.L.E. Agent Markers, THRUSH Chief Cards, THRUSH Agent Tokens.

PREPARATION

Shuffle all the THRUSH Chief Cards, and place one face down on each of the THRUSH Chief spaces on the Game Board. (Yellow illustrated areas.) Shuffle all the U.N.C.L.E. Assignment Cards. Deal 1 card face down to each player. Place the remaining cards in the Game Box. The Assignment Card dealt to each player is the THRUSH Chief he must capture.

Place one THRUSH Agent Token on each of the Intersections containing 4 arrows.

Each player selects a different colored U.N.C.L.E. Agent Marker and places it in the "Start" area.

Players toss the Dice. The highest number goes first, the player to his left will go second and so on.

STARTING THE GAME

The first player tosses the Dice. He moves his Marker along any starting path the full count of either die.

Example: The player throws a 5 and a 3 he cannot move 8 spaces. He may only move his Marker 5 spaces or 3 spaces.

If he throws a double, he must move his Marker the total of both Dice.

A player may move in only one direction either forward or backward during any one move. A player may not change paths unless he lands by an exact count on an intersection.

FIGHTING THRUSH AGENTS

When a player lands directly on an intersection occupied by a THRUSH Agent (Token) he must challenge the THRUSH Agent. This is done by immediately rolling one Die. If the player rolls a 1, 2, 3, or 4 he wins the challenge and captures the Agent and places the Token in front of him. If he rolls a 5 or 6, he loses the challenge and places his Marker immediately to THRUSH where it is, and move his Marker immediately to THRUSH Headquarters.

When a player lands on an unoccupied Intersection, he may move along any intersecting path on his next move.

GETTING OUT OF THRUSH HEADQUARTERS

A player imprisoned in THRUSH Headquarters must stay there 3 turns and then go back to "Start" unless he can do one of the following:

1. Throw a double and go back to "Start" at once.

2. Place a captured THRUSH Agent Token or a THRUSH Chief Card on an empty Intersection or empty Chief Space on the Game Board and go back to "Start" at once.

LOOKING AT THRUSH CHIEF CARDS

When a player lands directly on a Space marked with a Black Dot pointing to a Yellow THRUSH Chief Space, he may look at the Card on the space to see if it is the THRUSH Chief he is after.

CAPTURING THRUSH CHIEFS

When a player has captured 3 THRUSH Agents (Tokens), he may then capture a THRUSH Chief, by landing directly on a space pointing to a THRUSH Chief Card. The player after looking at the THRUSH Chief Card has his choice of either taking it or leaving it. If he takes the card, he must place his 3 captured THRUSH Agent Tokens on any 3 empty Intersections. A player may, in order to confuse the other players or prevent another

player from obtaining a card, take a THRUSH Chief Card even if it does not match his Assignment Card.

A player may never have more than 3 THRUSH Agent Tokens in his possession at any time. He may have as many THRUSH Chief Cards as he can capture.

Remember . . . in order to capture THRUSH Chief Cards, a player must have 3 THRUSH Agent Tokens in his possession.

CHANGING THRUSH CHIEF CARDS

When a player lands by an exact count on a space pointing to a THRUSH Chief Card, he may exchange any THRUSH card in his possession with the one on the Game Board.

RETURNING TO U.N.C.L.E. HEADQUARTERS

Once a player has a THRUSH Chief Card which matches his assignment card he must try to return to U.N.C.L.E. Headquarters at once. He cannot re-enter U.N.C.L.E. Headquarters through the front entrance (Starting position) he can only return through any of the 4 paths leading to the side entrances.

LANDING ON ANOTHER PLAYER

Whenever a player lands by an exact count on a space occupied by another player, he may do one of the followings:

Take one THRUSH Chief Card from the other player.

OR

Take one THRUSH Chief Card without looking at it from the other player. The player may only look at it after he has taken it. If the other player has neither Agent Tokens or Chief Cards, he is not penalized.

This is an important part of the game. If a player thinks another player has found his THRUSH Chief he should try to land on the same space as this player in order to take the card from him.

WINNING THE GAME

The first player to return to U.N.C.L.E. Headquarters with the THRUSH Chief Card which matches his Assignment Card, through the side entrance, wins the game.

© 1965 IDEAL TOY CORPORATION

Above and below: U.N.C.L.E. Board Game by Ideal.

Ideal U.N.C.L.E. Board Game, Canadian edition.

Illya Kuryakin Gun Set, Ideal Toys, 1966

Moving into 1966, Ideal continued to expand its toy range and with the increased popularity of David McCallum as Illya, the products reflected this, with Illya becoming more featured on packaging designs. One of the big toys released in 1966 was the Illya Kuryakin Gun set. This set featured a large clip-loading, cap-firing plastic pistol, which, like the Solo Gun before it, also saw rerelease in various other guises. This gun shares some similarity to a Broomhandle Mauser, but certainly no gun like this was ever featured in the series. Also included with this was the normal badge, wallet and ID card.

A second version of this set appeared with the outer ridge of the box looking similar to the first set but with a different backing card containing a small gun, holster and belt replacing the wallet included in the original set. The additional gun and holster appear to have come from the Stash-Away Gun set also issued by Ideal Toys in 1966.

Illya Kuryakin Gun set. (Warner Todd Huston collection)

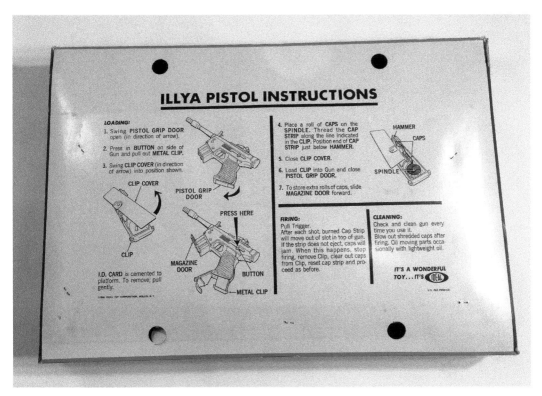

Illya Kuryakin Gun set box reverse. (Warner Todd Huston collection)

U.N.C.L.E. Stash-Away Gun set, Ideal trade catalogue advert.

U.N.C.L.E. Stash-Away Guns, Ideal Toys, 1966

Once again demonstrating his popularity, Illya is featured here prominently, demoting Solo to an almost secondary role on the packaging display. The set itself contained three small cap-firing guns with holsters, two straps, an ID card and the triangular badge. The guns in this set resembled miniature versions of a P38, a .45 and a Luger. The three small holsters in this set were in different coloured plastics, one each in black, blue and grey.

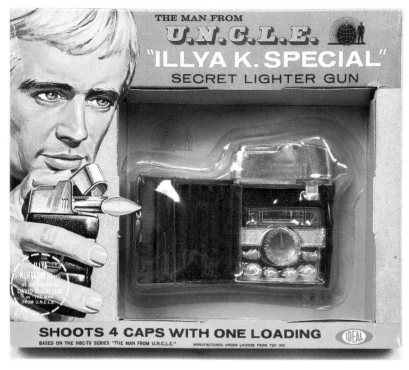

Left: Illya Kuryakin Special (Vectis).

Below left: Illya Kuryakin Special working features.

Below right: Illya Kuryakin Special with rare first issue internal sticker. (Warner Todd Huston collection)

Illya Kuryakin Special, Ideal Toys, 1966

Yet another toy focusing on Illya's popularity was this oversized cigarette lighter/cigarette case, which was in fact both a concealed gun and pocket radio. There are two issues of this model. The earliest comes in a 13-inch box, along with an illustration of Illya using the gun. It also featured a couple of illustrations of the toy itself. This first issue also features a sticker depicting the radio controls hidden in the secret compartment, while the later

The THRUSH Ray Gun Affair game.

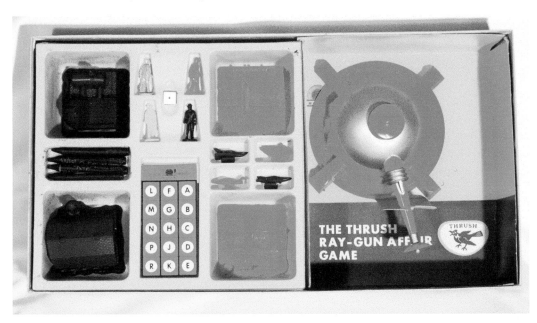

THRUSH Ray Gun Affair game contents.

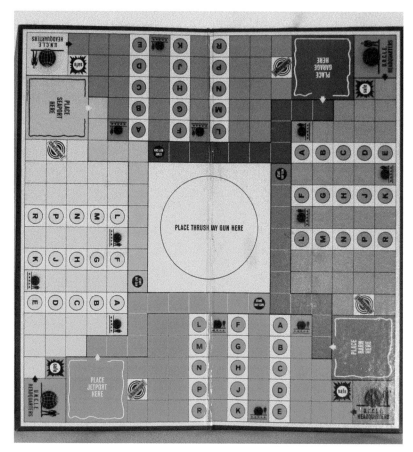

THRUSH Ray
Gun Affair
game board.

Above left: THRUSH Ray Gun Affair game red ray gun.

Above right: THRUSH Ray Gun Affair game blue ray gun. (Warner Todd Huston collection)

issue comes with a much narrower box and does not have the control panel sticker. This is a nice, robust toy around 3 to 4 inches in size, with a working cap gun built into the top section and a nice-looking moulded radio control panel behind a façade of fake cigarettes. According to the paper instructions, the central control dial could be removed to store caps.

The THRUSH Ray Gun Affair Game, Ideal Toys, 1966

Ideal Toys' next board game for the series was much nicer and far more complex than the previous one issued by the company. The game had nicely moulded playing pieces, including a very nice mechanically operated ray gun which would be placed in the middle of the playing board. Also included were four moulded buildings which represented different THRUSH hideouts. On the original Ideal sales sheets these are shown as being painted quite realistically, though when it came to the actual production run they were just moulded in a single colour of plastic to cut costs. This is another of those toys where you can find the plastic components in different colours, with some sets containing a red ray gun and others containing a blue one. This board game was quite expensive for the time with an issue price of $5.88 – only a few cents off the issue price of the THRUSH rifle, which Ideal also produced.

THRUSH Ray Gun Affair game, Ideal trade advert.

THRUSH gun. (David Oliver/www.moviebilia.co.uk collection)

THRUSH Gun, Ideal Toys, 1966

This has to be the star item of the whole Ideal Toys line of U.N.C.L.E. toys. Issued in 1966 and described on the packaging as a THRUSH gun, it is actually more accurately a 3-foot-long child's rife complete with a large 'infra-red sight'. Retailing at just under $6 ($5.99), this is probably one of the most sought-after and expensive U.N.C.L.E. toys to have been produced, with mint boxed examples having sold for $6,000 plus in recent years. As with the other Ideal guns, this featured the clip loading cap system. The scope had four silhouetted targets contained within it, which vanished when the rife was fired.

Also produced by Ideal was a child's wallet which featured a printed image of both Napoleon and Illya. These vinyl plastic wallets were available in either brown or blue. In addition, a small snap purse printed with an image of Illya was produced in either red or white vinyl. Due to the nature of these products, they are now almost impossible to find.

A few other items were produced and issued by Ideal, though not commercially, one of which was the U.N.C.L.E. Law Enforcement Manual. These activity books were sent in bulk to local TV stations carrying the series. The TV station would then send them out to young fans, along with photographs of Napoleon and Illya, who wrote into the station about the show. The manual also contained advertising for the toy line.

Above left: Child's wallet reverse. (Warner Todd Huston collection)

Above right: Childs wallet front. (Warner Todd Huston collection)

Snap purse, white. (Warner Todd Huston collection)

Above left: Snap purse, red. (Warner Todd Huston collection)

Above right: Snap purse, red reverse. (Warner Todd Huston collection)

Another promotional item produced by Ideal was a pair of flyers, one depicting Illya and the other depicting Solo, with the Ideal toy gun. It is believed that this item was sent out to toy buyers and store representatives with the aim of convincing them to stock the Ideal range of U.N.C.L.E. products. The highly touched-up photographs feature an illustrated gun which more closely represents both the Ideal toy gun and the original Mauser design from the series. These flyers are roughly A4, or more accurately are what they call standard letter-sized paper in the USA.

Best Wishes,
The Man from U.N.C.L.E.
Illya Kuryakin

OFFICIAL Man from U.N.C.L.E. gun . . . only by Ideal
It's a wonderful gun . . . . . . it's (IDEAL)

Promotional flyer for Illya. (Warner Todd Huston collection)

Lone Star Badge No. 2 on backing card. (Vectis)

Chapter Three
Man from U.N.C.L.E.
Lone Star Range

Lone Star Toys, the trade name used by Die-Cast Machine Tools Ltd (DCMT) for their toy division, was probably the largest producer of U.N.C.L.E.-related toys in the UK, producing numerous gun sets and attaché cases starting in 1965.

The cheapest and probably one of the most popular items in their range would have been the U.N.C.L.E. ID badge. Unlike Ideal's US toys, where the ID badges were only produced with a number six on them and were never sold separately, in the UK Lone Star sold the badges individually from a shop display backing card of twelve badges. Like the US toys, Lone Star also included a badge in their larger U.N.C.L.E. sets.

The Lone Star badges featured either a '2' or '11' – Illya and Napoleon's numbers respectively. As stated, these were sold loose from a backing cardboard sheet which featured a cut-out U.N.C.L.E. badge (triangular) showing a number eleven. This backing card had a large U.N.C.L.E. logo in the bottom right corner, with the cut-out badge and a photo of Solo above that. To the left is a photo of Illya on a yellow background. At first you could be excused for thinking it strange that a backing card for loose badges should

Above left: Lone Star Badge No. 11 on backing card. (Vectis)

Above right: Standard Lone Star backing card.

Badge comparison: embossed badge from Lone Star case and non-embossed example as sold loose.

also feature a cut-out badge, but this backing card was also used for several other Lone Star-issued U.N.C.L.E. products.

The badges sold loose from these backing cards appear to have been flat-printed, while those badges that originated from within one of the Lone Star-produced sets were slightly embossed. The above photograph shows the distinct difference between the badges Lone Star produced.

Lone Star Mauser.

Next up from Lone Star is the Mauser Pistol 7.63 mm Automatic. This die-cast metal gun was issued in a dark blue/grey almost black colour with a red plastic grip and was capable of firing the old-fashioned 100 shot role caps so beloved of toy gun producers. The 7.63 mm automatic by Lone Star was based on the 1934 7.65mm German Mauser, though a Mauser was used in the early first season episodes. This one was based on a different design of Mauser, which in the series was soon to be replaced by a specially adapted Walther P38, due to several reasons both technical and cost wise. The Lone Star model was a fairly accurate replica that could be bought either separately or in any one of several sets, with various attachments etc.

 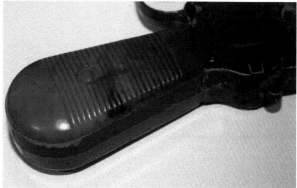

Above left, right and below: Lone Star Mauser attachment points comparison.

Mauser with holster.

It is interesting to note that the Mauser can also be found in two different versions: one with attachment points for shoulder stock and gun sight, and the other without.

The Mauser is also the only one of the Lone Star-produced U.N.C.L.E. guns to have 'U.N.C.L.E.' embossed on the side. The other guns produced by Lone Star just had small stickers stating 'U.N.C.L.E.' on the side. These were originally priced at 6s 11d in the UK.

Pistol with Holster and Silencer, Lone Star, 1965

The Mauser was also issued with a plastic silencer and holster. Issued on the same backing card as the badges, these were sold at the princely sum of 12s 6d. (How the price of nearly double could be justified for the addition of a plastic silencer and a holster is anyone's guess!) All holsters should have a loop to the side which contained the silencer, but sadly that has been torn off on the example photographed above.

Once again there does seem to be variations with the holster. Some have a white U.N.C.L.E. badge/logo printed on them, while some have this same badge/logo but printed in gold. From the examples that have been seen while carrying out the research for this book, it would appear that the gold-printed holsters were issued in the attaché cases while the white-printed holsters were issued on backing cards with the gun.

Holster comparison.

Luger pistol.

Luger Pistol, Lone Star, 1968

To save costs, in 1968 Lone Star replaced several character guns in their range with standard Luger pistols, which with the addition of a small paper sticker could be made to represent any TV series. The same Luger model was used for at least U.N.C.L.E., *Bond* and *The Saint*. This version was sold as an U.N.C.L.E. special on the same backing card that had been used for the badges. This gun was also sold with a holster and plastic silencer, once again on the same backing card.

The original Mauser pistol was also part of a mail-in offer through *TV21*, being one of several different toy guns that could be purchased through the comic. Included in the offer were a 'Secret Agent 21' holster and silencer. There seems to be some debate on whether this was an U.N.C.L.E. issue or not, and I have not yet found any actual mention of U.N.C.L.E. appearing within the offer in *TV21* comic, though the series did feature in issues of its sister comic, *Lady Penelope*.

TV21 comic offer.

Combination rifle.

Lady Penelope comic with U.N.C.L.E. cover.

Combination rifle case showing wrap-around label. (David Oliver/www.moviebilia.co.uk collection)

Assembled rifle.

Combination Rifle, AKA Small Attaché Case, Lone Star, 1965

Once again the Mauser 7.63 mm automatic is featured, this time with a plastic silencer, sights and a part-metal/part-plastic shoulder stock. It was all contained in a black cardboard suitcase with a polystyrene inlay. When assembled any budding young secret agent would feel the part with this nicely made toy gun. This example from the David Oliver/www.moviebilia.co.uk collection shows the extremely rare paper label that surrounded the case. The reverse of this showed instructions of how you should assemble the rife. Similar paper labels originally surrounded all of the different-sized cases that Lone Star produced for U.N.C.L.E. Of the different U.N.C.L.E. cases produced by the firm, this is the only one of the Lone Star sets that seems to have remained consistent throughout its production run; all of the other sets seem to have constantly changed contents throughout their run.

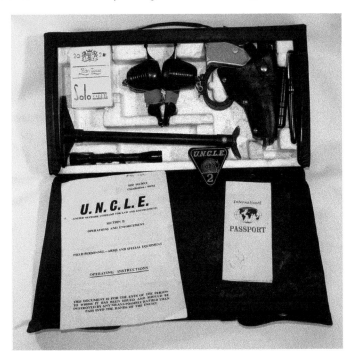

U.N.C.L.E. Agents Field Kit.

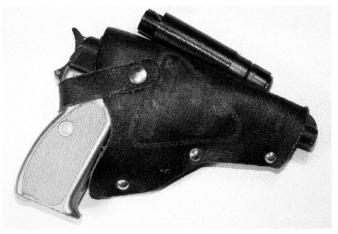

Gun in holster.

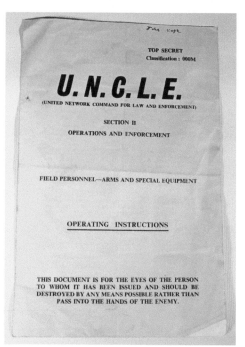

Above left: Vosene advert from *TV21*.

Above right: Agent Field Kit leaflet.

U.N.C.L.E. Agents Field Kit, AKA Medium Attaché Case, Lone Star, 1966

This first issue of the Medium Attaché contained the Lone Star Mauser gun in a black suitcase, which was constructed from PVC-bound cardboard and sized around 15 inches by 8 inches and around 2½ inches deep. Along with the aforementioned Mauser pistol, the polystyrene-formed interior contained a plastic silencer, holster, shoulder stock and a plastic sight. Also included were a triangular badge, an U.N.C.L.E. pen with ink, an intercom set, handcuffs, a passport, a white plastic cigarette packet (the label on which reads 'Solo Cigarettes') and a pocket radio set, plus a small chrome-plated pistol. The pen contained in all the Lone Star U.N.C.L.E. sets was the invisible writing fountain pen produced by Platignum.

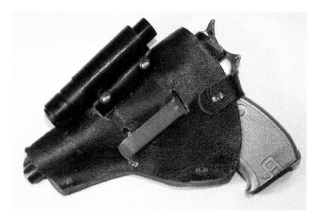

Rear of holster showing belt clip.

P38 gun.

Handcuffs.

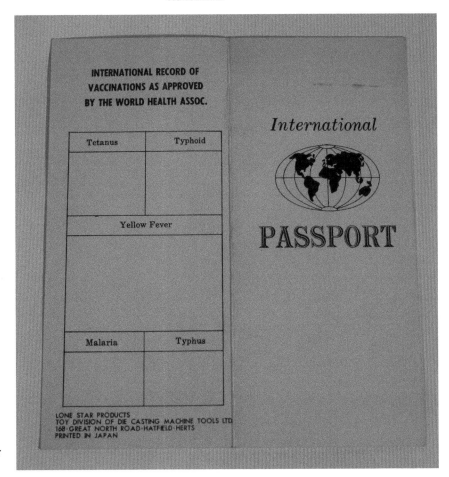

Lone Star
Passport.

U.N.C.L.E. Agents Field Kit, AKA Medium Attaché Case, Lone Star, 1968

This second issue of the set is near identical in contents to the earlier issue, apart for the substitution of a Walther P38 for the Mauser. A special offer for this latter issue set was promoted on Vosene shampoo and Macleans toothpaste packaging.

Of note is that the Solo Cigarettes that were issued in this medium-sized case were also sold loose on a backing card but not as a U.N.C.L.E. product.

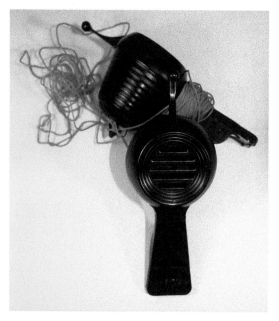

Above left: Walkie-talkies.

Above right: Solo Cigarettes.

Above left: Solo Cigarettes showing concealed gun.

Above right: First issue large case catalogue detail.

Attaché Case, AKA Large Attaché Case, Lone Star, 1966

The Large Attaché Case set varied a lot in contents and layout. The contents were placed in a black suitcase that was constructed from PVC-bound cardboard and was around 17 inches by 12 inches and 2½ inches deep. According to the 1966 Lone Star catalogue, the

Above and below: Large case variation.

Large case
variation.
(All Vectis)

first issue of this set contained the Mauser pistol with all attachments, the holster and the walkie-talkie set. These Lone Star walkie-talkies worked on the infamous tin can with a bit of string principle. Also included were a grenade, atomising camera, pen, decoder, wallet, secret pistol and a badge. This had an original issue price of £3 4s 6d.

Attaché Case, Aka Large Attaché Case, Lone Star, 1968

This is the most inconsistent of Lone Star's U.N.C.L.E. sets with at least five different box layouts or variations of contents having been witnessed during research for this book. Firstly, the basic set included a black suitcase that was constructed from PVC-bound cardboard and was around 17 inches by 12 inches and 2½ inches deep. According to the Lone Star catalogue, the 1968 issue of this set appears to have contained the Luger pistol with all attachments, the holster, walkie-talkie, grenade, Solo Cigarettes, the secret pistol, a pen, decoder, wallet and a badge.

Above left: Luger's embossed side.

Above right: Luger reverse.

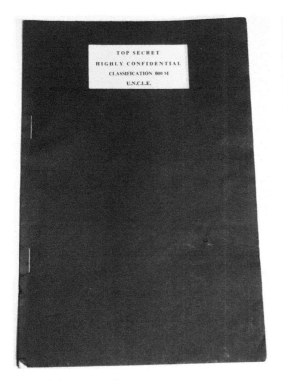

Above left: Manual from large case.

Above right: Wallet.

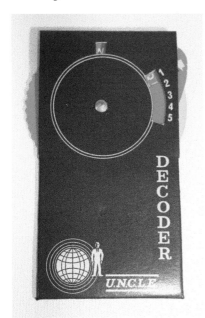
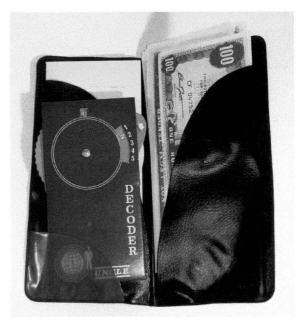

Above left: Secret message decoder.

Above right: Wallet with contents.

Holster with belt.

Lone Star cases size
comparison.

Cartridge pen.

Another version was closer to the original issue, containing the Luger pistol with all attachments: the holster, walkie-talkie set, a grenade, atomising camera, pen, decoder, wallet, secret pistol and a badge. While a third incomplete set shows a different tray layout, since the instruction book is missing, it is difficult to assess how different the contents where in relation to other sets.

A fourth version of this later issue set shows even more variation in the layout and contents of the set, along with a different Lone Star Lugar, though as the set is incomplete it is possible that an earlier standard-issue Lone Star Luger was substituted. This Luger has no U.N.C.L.E. paper label, but instead has 'Lugar' embossed on to the side of the gun.

U.N.C.L.E Invisible Writing Cartridge Pen, Platignum, 1965

While on the subject of the Lone Star cases, this seems the appropriate place to mention one of the standard components: the pen. Marketed individually by Platignum, the top of the pen is marked with ridges to represent a microphone, while the cap had 'U.N.C.L.E.' lettered in silver on its side. The pen came with a total of four ink cartridges: two of a heat-activated invisible ink and two of normal ink. The pen was packaged on a card with the cartridges

Cartridge pen on
display card.

LOADING INSTRUCTIONS FOR THE PLATIGNUM 'UNCLE' PEN

It is important to note that there are two nib units supplied with this pen . . . one to be used for 'Invisible' Ink cartridges and one to be used for standard blue ink cartridges. Once the nib units have been put to use, they should only be applied to the original ink cartridge, that is to say, you should not fit 'Invisible' Ink cartridges to units which have been used for the Coloured Ink Cartridges and vice versa.

To fit a Cartridge:

1. Remove cap.
2. Unscrew barrel and insert open end of cartridge (after removing plastic plug) into nib section.
3. Replace barrel and screw up firmly.
4. Should ink not flow freely (this applies particularly to a new pen) unscrew barrel and "squeeze" the cartridge until a trace of ink can be seen on the nib point.
5. When replacing an empty ink cartridge, unscrew barrel and remove old cartridge with a slight unscrewing action.

Plastic plugs, supplied with each 'Invisible' Ink Cartridge, should be preserved so that if you wish to change over from Coloured Ink to 'Invisible' Ink or vice versa, you can plug a partly used cartridge which may then be stored safely. TO ENSURE THAT YOUR INVISIBLE WRITING IS REALLY SECRET ONLY VERY SLIGHT PRESSURE SHOULD BE APPLIED TO THE PAPER OTHERWISE A READABLE IMPRESSION WILL BE MADE. Having allowed the 'Invisible' Ink to dry, the writing is revealed by applying gentle heat to the underside of paper on which it is written. A feature of this 'Invisible' Ink is that having been made 'visible' it will slowly fade but a fresh application of gentle heat will reveal the writing again. If you are without a spare Coloured Ink Cartridge and your pen runs dry you can refill your pen by the following method:-

Remove the barrel, dip the nib into the ink, squeeze the cartridge case repeatedly between fore-finger and thumb and then release whilst the nib point is still in the ink. It will take in sufficient ink for emergency use.

From time to time it is important to clean your Cartridge Pen in order to ensure smooth writing. This is easily done by removing the Cartridge and holding the nib section under running water. After flushing thoroughly, dry by shaking off the excess moisture and replace cartridge.

CHOICE OF NIB UNITS AVAILABLE

Fine   Broad   Medium

Cartridge pen display card reverse. (Warner Todd Huston collection)

46

bubble-packed on. A spare nib for use with the normal ink was also included on the card. The pen was placed to the left side of the card with the logo above and 'U.N.C.L.E.' printed at the top and the cartridges were placed at the bottom with the spare nib just above and to the left. The pen came in several different colours, including red, black, light grey and midnight blue. Original priced at 6s 3d, it was later increasing to 6s 6d.

A couple of items that seem to fit into this section most neatly are the water pistol and the time bomb.

The water pistol, embossed with 'U.N.C.L.E.' on the side, appears to be based loosely upon a Smith & Wesson handgun. While there are no identifying manufacturer's details to be found anywhere on the piece, it is believed that it was produced by Carolina Enterprises Corp. as they held a licence in the USA to produce water pistols from the series. Anglo Centrop Ltd also apparently held a licence for water pistols in the UK. It is unknown if this was the same item issued in the UK under licence, but it seems probable.

The time bomb, while known to exist, was long believed to have been produced by Lone Star, as Lone Star did produce a die-cast time bomb similar to this. However, this toy is plastic with a tin baseplate, the die-cast component being the spring-loaded metal firing hammer. This used the standard 100-shot role caps readily available at the time and was issued on a red and black backing card by Merit Toys.

Above left: Water pistol.

Above right: Time bomb.

Above left: Time bomb workings.

Above right: Time bomb baseplate.

Chapter Four
The Gilbert Range

Gilbert Toys were another of the key manufacturers of U.N.C.L.E. toys in the USA, producing action figures and accessories for the series in 1965, along with several other products. The company is nowadays most known among TV/film toy collectors for its Sears-exclusive James Bond Road Race set, produced in 1965 – a toy which ultimately caused the company to go into liquidation. They were bought out by Ideal Toys, who continued to produce and market products under the Gilbert brand.

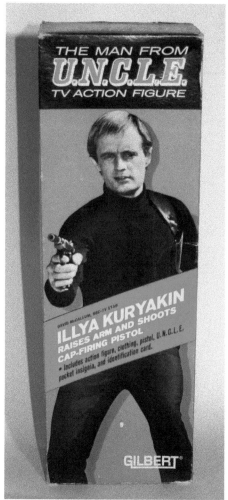

Above: Illya box.

Left: Illya doll.

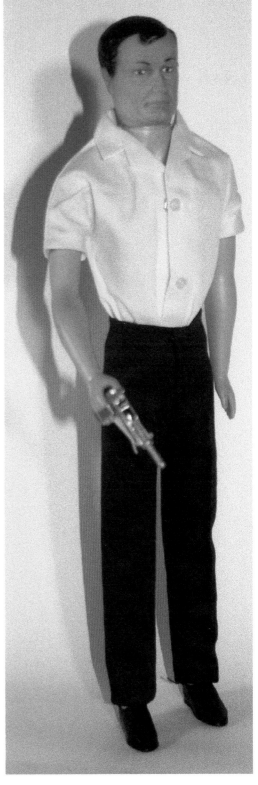

Above: Solo box.

Right: Solo doll.

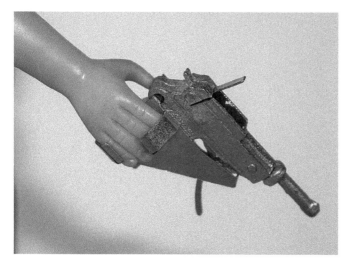

Left: Solo doll with working cap gun.

Below: Instructions for Gilbert action figures with ID badge and card.

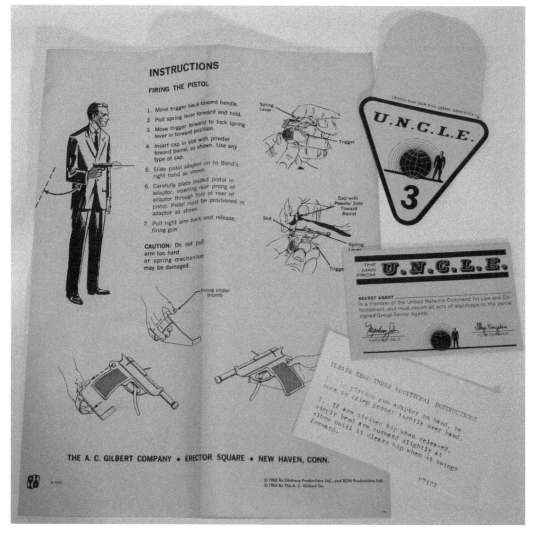

50

Gilbert Toys catalogue.

Illya hand puppet.

Illya hand puppet back.

Inside the image:

Famous Spy ACTION PUPPETS

Beautifully detailed miniatures of 4 famous movie and TV spy figures . . . molded in soft, pliable vinyl material for realistic action . . . 13 to 14 inches high, with completely molded body, legs, arms.

No. 16604 LARGO ACTION PUPPET. Newest and toughest villain in the James Bond movie rogues' gallery — from "Thunderball". Packed 12 to carton, shipping weight 8 lbs.

No. 16603 ILLYA KURYAKIN ACTION PUPPET. Colorful blond spy on "The Man From U.N.C.L.E." Packed 12 per carton, shipping weight 8 lbs.

Each puppet perfectly sca for child-size hand—but e grown-ups love 'em!

EW!
MMY
RNER
TION
ZZLES

adds
ACTION to
ool-age
!

Gilbert puppets in catalogue.

Issued at an original price of $2.99, Gilbert produced 12-inch action figures of both Napoleon Solo and Illya Kuryakin. Both of these came with spring-loaded arms that flipped up, enabling them to fire miniature working cap guns. The Gilbert catalogue describes the Napoleon Solo figure as a 'Superbly-modelled likeness of the man U.N.C.L.E. sends in when things get rough'. The figure is actually anything but a good likeness! The Napoleon figure came dressed in white shirt with black trousers and black shoes, though, as with almost all figures issued by this company, there tends to be some variation of costume. Some issues had plain black shoes, others had black and white shoes. Meanwhile, the Illya Kuryakin figure is dressed in a black polo-neck sweater with black trousers and black shoes. Included with both figures was a small cap-firing gun, an U.N.C.L.E. membership card and a paper ID badge.

A whole range of accessory sets was produced for these figures, though very few individual items, as the same pieces of equipment appear in multiple different sets (including sets for the James Bond and Honey West dolls also issued by the firm). The bulk of these sets came in tray-like boxes. It is not uncommon for many of these sets to turn up mint on the backing card, but minus the outer tray box.

While these action figures were certainly the main sellers for Gilbert, they did release other products.

Target Set, Gilbert Toys, 1965

This sold at an original price of $2.69 and included a 'bulletproof' vest, three targets with stands, an Action Bazooka that fires three harmless shells (also included) and working binoculars.

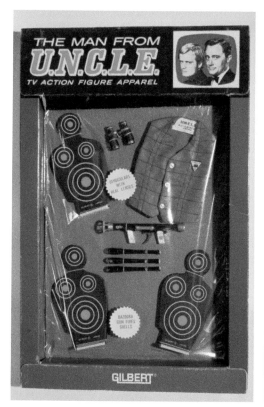 

Above left: Target set.

Above right: Armament set.

Armament Set, Gilbert Toys, 1965

Also at an original cost of $2.69 was the Armament set, which included and all-weather jacket, military beret, cap-firing pistol with four special attachments (barrel extension, bipod stand, rifle butt and telescopic sight), a knife, working binoculars, an accessory belt with a utility pouch and four grenades.

Scuba Set, Gilbert Toys, 1965

Once again priced at an original cost of $2.69, the Scuba set provided 'complete, authentically designed equipment to prepare U.N.C.L.E. agents for underwater espionage'. Included was a scuba jacket, swim trunks, air tanks, tank bracket, tubes and knife. All of these pieces also formed the basis for several of the accessory sets produced by Gilbert for its James Bond figure.

Jumpsuit Set, Gilbert Toys, 1965

Slightly more expensive at an original price of $2.99 was the Jumpsuit set. Included in this set was not only a complete jumpsuit with boots and helmet with chin strap, but also a 28-inch-diameter working parachute with a pack. A cap-firing Tommy Gun with a scope completed the set.

Scuba set.

Jumpsuit set.

Arsenal set 1.

Arsenal set 2.

Arsenal Set 1, Gilbert Toys, 1965

Gilbert produced two different Arsenal sets for the U.N.C.L.E. figures. The first came in a tray box and contained a spring-action bazooka with three shells, a cap-firing high-powered rifle and a cap-firing demountable gun with attachments for converting it to a rifle.

Arsenal Set 2, Gilbert Toys, 1965

The two other sets produced by Gilbert Toys were both available at an original issue price of $1.29. The first was the second Arsenal set, which contained a cap-firing THRUSH rifle with a telescopic sight, a grenade belt and four grenades.

Pistol Conversion Set, Gilbert Toys, 1965

The final accessory set was the Pistol Conversion set, which contained all the parts necessary to make the cap-firing pistol into an U.N.C.L.E. rifle, including a bipod, rifle butt, barrel extension and telescopic sight. This set also included working binoculars.

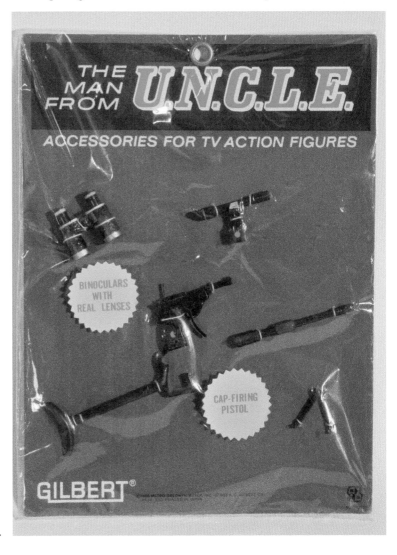

Pistol conversion set.

Hand grenade comparison: Gilbert grenade on left, Action Man/GI Joe grenade on right.

Illya Kuryakin Rubber Hand Puppet, Gilbert Toys, 1965

This soft plastic hand puppet came dressed in a black roll-neck sweater (what else?). Ever with an eye to marketing, the show's producer, Norman Felton, had even issued a memo in April 1965 to the production, stating: 'Please be sure to see that Illya uses turtleneck shirts and sweaters (costume department man will know what kind I'm referring to) next season.' Henceforth most models or images of Illya on products featured him in his almost trademark turtleneck shirt, this hand puppet being no exception. There appear to be two different issues of this puppet, as it has been found with either white or blue trousers. The figure is depicted holding a communicator in its left hand and is around 13 inches high. It originally came on a 16-inch by 10-inch backing card. As a puppet this figure had very limited flexibility and probably very limited play value to a child who no doubt preferred one of the action figures the company produced instead, though this didn't dissuade Gilbert from also issuing similar James Bond puppets.

Spy Magic Tricks, Gilbert Toys, 1965

This is quite an unusual item from Gilbert and is a prime example of toy companies trying to sell any old product by slapping a character theme onto it. Marketed at an original price of $2.99, this is a very basic children's magic set repackaged to have a spy theme.

Right: Spy magic.

Below: Spy magic contents.

Seven tricks were included, all with the word 'affair' added to the name of the item. Tricks included 'The Baffling THRUSH Card Affair', 'The Astonishing Magic Money Affair', 'The Incredible Mystery Gun Affair' (the only thing incredible about this trick is how anyone could ever be fooled by it), 'The Puzzling Spy Tag Affair', 'The Strange Lie Detector Affair', 'The Odd Vanishing Key Affair' and the 'Amazing X-Ray Scope Affair'. We could elaborate more on these wondrous feats of magic, but why risk the wrath of the Magic Circle for revealing their tricks. Go to the joke shop down the road and buy them yourself – you'll get the same tricks for a lot less than buying this set nowadays.

Chapter Five
Louis Marx Products

American toy giant Louis Marx was another producer of several U.N.C.L.E. toys, introducing several products during 1966.

One of the star items in the Marx range of U.N.C.L.E. toys was the Target set sold exclusively through Sears and Roebuck stores for $3.99. This came packaged in a plain brown cardboard box marked with 'MAN FROM UNCLE TARGET SET' in red across the centre of the box. The set contains two dart-firing pistols and twelve approximately 6-inch-high plastic figures. Six darts and two message grenades were also included for use with the pistols along with an instruction sheet detailing how the large (54-inch by 17-inch) cardboard backdrop/buildings should be assembled. The plastic figures included consisted of three U.N.C.L.E. and three THRUSH agents in blue plastic and six brown plastic generic agents. All of the plastic figures sold within this set were also available through the stores for 10¢ each. At the time these figures were only produced in these colours, the exception being the figures of Napoleon and Illya, which were also produced in grey plastic. The three U.N.C.L.E. agent figures produced were Napoleon Solo, Illya Kuryakin and Mr Waverley.

Marx Target set. (Warner Todd Huston collection)

Above left: Marx Solo figure.

Above right: Marx Illya figure.

Right: Marx Mr Waverly figure.

Above left: Marx THRUSH officer.

Above right: Marx THRUSH Agent 1.

Left: Marx THRUSH Agent 2.

Marx generic agent.

Meanwhile, the THRUSH agents were named 'THRUSH Agent 1' (aiming a THRUSH rifle), 'THRUSH Agent 2' (shooting a pistol in his left hand) and 'THRUSH Officer' (with a gun in his right hand). These six figures were only produced in blue plastic, aside from the aforementioned Napoleon and Illya figures. The other six figures have no markings on them that connect them to the series other than the fact that they were contained within the U.N.C.L.E. Target set. These six figures were only issued in brown plastic. In recent years several of these figures have appeared on various internet sales sites in many different colours, being cited as rare prototype models. The simple fact is that the original moulds for these figures are still in existence and some enterprising individual is reproducing these figures in strange colours. Sadly, the only available examples for photographing in this book of some of these figures were reissues in silver plastic.

Secret Code Wheel Box.

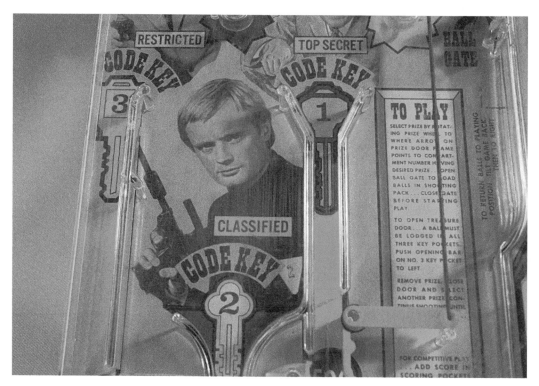

The text visible within the image includes:

RESTRICTED
CODE KEY 3

TOP SECRET
CODE KEY 1

BALL GATE

CLASSIFIED
CODE KEY 2

TO PLAY

SELECT PRIZE BY ROTAT-
ING PRIZE WHEEL TO
WHERE ARROW ON
PRIZE DOOR FRAME
POINTS TO COMPART-
MENT NUMBER HAVING
DESIRED PRIZE... OPEN
BALL GATE TO LOAD
BALLS IN SHOOTING
PACK... CLOSE GATE
BEFORE STARTING
PLAY.

TO OPEN TREASURE
DOOR... A BALL MUST
BE LODGED IN ALL
THREE KEY POCKETS.
PUSH OPENING BAR
ON NO. 3 KEY POCKET
TO LEFT.

REMOVE PRIZE, CLOSE
DOOR AND SELECT
ANOTHER PRIZE CON-
TINUE SHOOTING UNTIL

FOR COMPETITIVE PLAY
... ADD SCORE IN
SCORING POCKETS

TO RETURN BALLS TO PLAYING
POSITION, TILT GAME BACK
THEN TO RIGHT

Above and below: Secret Code Wheel detail.

SECRET CODE WHEEL
THE MAN FROM U.N.C.L.E.

Secret Code Wheel detail.

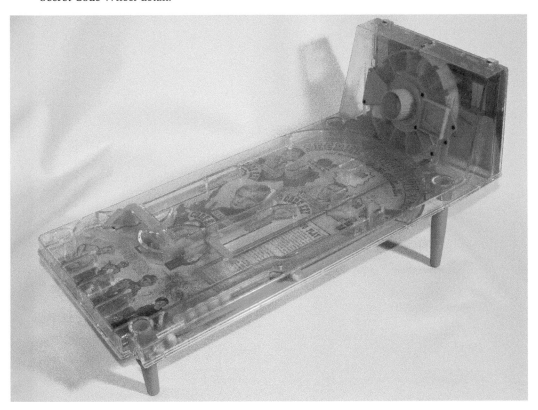

Secret Code Wheel.

Secret Code Wheel Pinball Game, Marx, 1966

Sears also had a second item made exclusively for them by Louis Marx: the Secret Code Wheel Pinball Game. This pinball game was a little elaborate; it had a code wheel at one end that could be accessed if you managed to get three marbles into the correct positions on the pinball machine, enabling the lock on the code wheel to release and thus providing access to several small plastic prizes. This is quite a large piece at just under 2 feet long and features a nicely illustrated tin-litho baseplate.

Pinball Game, Marx, 1966

Marx also produced a slightly smaller and more basic pinball game that was marketed as 'The Pinball Affair'. This basic pinball game was sold under many different guises. Seeing as the plastic components had nothing specific to any subject, Marx was able

Above left: Pinball game.

Above right: Cane pistol. (Warner Todd Huston collection)

to just exchange the printed tin-litho in order to market it as a different game – a very common practice among toy manufacturers. It appears to have been sold loose with no outer packaging.

While on the subject of pinball games, a third pinball game was produced, though not by Marx, and was sold as a bagatelle game. It was produced in Hong Kong in 1966 for sale in the UK and other Commonwealth countries, and was packaged in a display box. However, at present the manufacturer of these is unknown.

U.N.C.L.E. Cane Pistol, Marx, 1966

The cane pistol was just over 2 feet long and was able to fire caps and a small plastic bullet. The cane came on a fully illustrated backing card and the production of this item was no doubt influenced by the use of a similar style gadget by one of the chief villains in the second season episode 'The Re-Collectors Affair'. The cane was marketed with eight small plastic bullets and a small shell casing into which the cap and bullets would be placed for firing. This originally sold for just under a dollar at 95¢.

Marx also produced two different shooting arcades in 1966. The gun on the larger of the two had both the shoulder stock and scope to its gun while the smaller was just

Large Shooting Arcade. (Warner Todd Huston collection)

Small Shooting Arcade box. (Warner Todd Huston collection)

a basic pistol. These were fully enclosed Shooting Arcades, ensuring that the pellets fired could neither get lost nor cause any damage, other than where intended. The large version had a mechanical rotating target while the smaller economy version just had spinning targets.

Counterspy Outfit, Marx, 1966

Marx's Counterspy Outfit included a variety of different plastic gadgets as well as a child's waterproof trench coat. Included was a plastic pistol complete with a detachable scope,

Counterspy outfit box.

Rare UK Counterspy Outfit.

shoulder stock and extended barrel. This was capable of firing missiles that were included. Plastic beards, moustaches and glasses were some of the disguise items within the set, along with a small make-up pallet. The most fun items in the set though were the knife (which had a hidden gun), exploding cigarette case and exploding grenade.

The set was produced in several different sizes for different age ranges and boxes were colour-coded depending upon the size of child the set was intended for. The set intended for five to six year olds came in a pale green box, with a larger size for nine to ten year olds coming in a pale blue box. Whatever sized child the set was for, the basic contents of each set remained the same. The original USA issue of these sets was priced at $7.29 and came in a box that featured photographic images of Napoleon and Illya. Strangely, the UK issue of these sets featured artwork that was crude in comparison.

Bicycle Licence Plates, Marx, 1967

Another product from Marx was a set of four different pressed tin licence plates intended for children's bicycles. These were sold individually in a small plastic bag with a header card. Each plate featured the U.N.C.L.E. logo, with one being a generic plate for the series, one having Napoleon Solo's name, one having Illya Kuryakin and the final one bearing the name of *The Girl from U.N.C.L.E.*

According to information in the press book for the double bill cinema release of *To Trap a Spy* and *The Spy with My Face*, Marx did hold a licence for two other products. One was a Flashy Flicker Gun and the other a Speedway Road Racing set. However, it appears that neither product was actually produced.

Counterspy Outfit contents.

Make-up kit.

Gun and holster.

Counterspy kit contents.

Exploding items from Counterspy set.

Napoleon Solo bicycle licence plate.

70

Chapter Six
Model Cars

THRUSH-Buster in dark blue.

Corgi advert.

On the back of their success in marketing models of the Saint's Volvo P1800 and James Bond's Aston Martin DB5, Corgi Toys in the UK turned its eyes towards the American market. Choosing a pre-existing typical American car from its range, the company turned a basic Oldsmobile into the U.N.C.L.E. THRUSH-Buster.

THRUSH-Buster white.

THRUSH-Buster
comparison:
dark blue with
lighter blue
at bottom.

U.N.C.L.E. THRUSH-Buster, Corgi Toys No. 497, 1966

There are several different original variations of this model, though there are now a vast range of strangely coloured, repainted Code 3 models. For those not initiated, a Code 3 model is an original item that has been repainted or customised without the knowledge or consent of the original manufacturer.

The THRUSH-Buster was based upon a 1961 Oldsmobile Super 88 Sedan. Inside sat small figures of Napoleon and Illya, which, when the button on the top was depressed, would lean out alternately and appear to fire their guns with a clicking sound. The button was meant to represent some sort of rear-facing periscope. On all versions the bonnet of the model is white with the U.N.C.L.E. logo.

Above:
THRUSH-Buster baseplate.

Right: Original Waverly ring showing Solo.

Original Waverly ring showing Illya.

At present four different original versions are known. The first and possibly most common version was dark blue with grey metal spotlights attached to the bonnet. The second, almost identical issue featured 'chromed' plastic spotlights as opposed to the metal ones of the previous issue. The third version of this model was the one that stands out the most, being white (well, to be more precise an off-white/cream colour). Like the first dark blue issue, it had metal spotlights. Finally, there was a light blue version of the car which featured chromed plastic spotlights. How rare or not this particular version is, is hard to determine and it is very nearly identical to the dark blue issues. It is only when placed next to the regular blue issue that the difference in colour becomes apparent. In fact, it was at first believed that it may just have been a slightly faded standard issue, but close inspection of the model proves this not to be the case.

All issues of this model came with a small plastic 'Waverly' ring, named after Napoleon and Illya's boss in the series. This ring, depending on which way it was tilted, showed either a picture of Napoleon or Illya. Beware, however, as there are very good reproductions of this ring on the market. The easiest way to tell an original ring from the reproduction is to look at the photograph of Illya. If this picture depicts Illya wearing a polo then it's most likely a reproduction, as on the original Illya has a normal shirt collar. The images on the original rings also have much less background than the later reproductions. In the UK these models were marketed at an original price of 8s 11d, while in the USA it would have cost you $2.75.

U.N.C.L.E. Piranha Car, Husky (Corgi), 1966

In the mid-1960s Corgi Toys signed a deal with F. W. Woolworths to produce an exclusive range of pocket-money toy cars of a similar size to the Matchbox models. These were marketed under the brand name Husky, and while most of these were just ordinary vehicles, Corgi did introduce a range of what were known as Husky Extras. This range

Above: AMT Piranha kit.

Right: Husky USA first issue. (Vectis)

Husky UK first issue. (Vectis)

Husky USA second issue. (Vectis)

Corgi Juniors USA issue card.

Loose Husky Piranha car.

Husky/Corgi baseplate comparison.

featured vehicles that had a little extra play-value as it were. Among this range was the only diecast version of the U.N.C.L.E. Piranha sports car – a car which, unlike the fictional THRUSH-Buster, did actually appear in the series.

The Piranha sports car was introduced during the series' third season and was built by famed custom car designer Gene Winfield. The car, based on a Corvair, was already being developed and tried out around drag races in the USA prior to the U.N.C.L.E. version built by Winfield and AMT. This is another great example of how the series worked with toy companies in marketing the series, because with AMT being involved in the vehicle's real-life production, the car would go on the market as a plastic kit.

Both the Husky and later Corgi Juniors versions were a pale blue in colour, like the one featured in the show. These small models were able to fire a plastic missile from their bonnet and featured miniature figures of Napoleon and Illya seated inside. All of the different issues of this model appear to be the same; the only differences are the printed backing cards.

This first issue of the model is numbered as Husky No. 1005 and can be found with the printed price of either 59¢ or 3s 3d depending on whether they were purchased from a UK or USA store. Otherwise, both are identical.

The following year's issue featured a printed price of 69¢. The Husky number also changed; the original 1005 was struck through and a new 1205 replaced it.

U.N.C.L.E. Piranha Car, Corgi Juniors, 1970
This model followed the end of the exclusively produced Husky range for F. W. Woolworths in 1970. The models produced for that range were repackaged as Corgi Juniors, and for the large part the models had both whizz-wheels fitted and the Husky name removed from the baseplate. This model from the Husky range seems to have escaped that, with a small paper label proclaiming 'Corgi Toys' instead being stuck over the Husky logo on the model's baseplate. The model also had another price increase in the USA, now being sold at 75¢.

Crime Busters Gift Set, Husky, 1967
Not shy at trying to maximise sales, the Piranha was also featured in a boxed set of vehicles sold as the Crime Busters gift set. This set of four also featured models of James Bond's Aston Martin, the Batmobile and the Batboat. Once again, this set can be found issued by both Husky and later on by Corgi Toys.

Husky Crime Busters set. (Vectis)

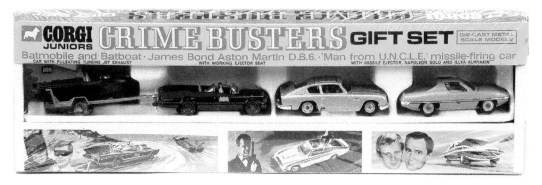

Corgi Crime Busters set. (Vectis)

Playart U.N.C.L.E. car. (Warner Todd Huston collection)

U.N.C.L.E. Car, Playart, 1968

Unusually, while other firms were winding down production of U.N.C.L.E. toys, Playart, a Hong Kong firm, decided to produce its own U.N.C.L.E. car. Similar in size and appearance to the Corgi THRUSH-Buster, Playart's U.N.C.L.E. car features none of the working features of its Corgi counterpart and it appears to have been produced in a wide variety of colours. Normally sold individually on a plain backing card, the only thing tying the model to the series is the word 'U.N.C.L.E.' cast into the model's baseplate. This model has also been seen packaged with another ordinary vehicle on a plain backing card.

Playart baseplate. (Warner Todd Huston collection)

Friction-driven U.N.C.L.E. car from South America.

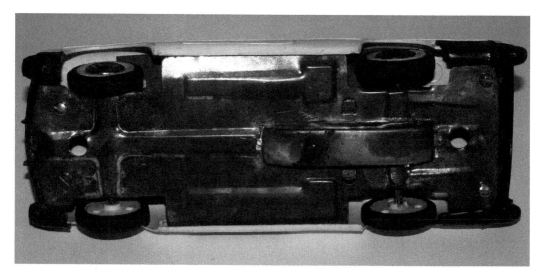

Friction-driven car base.

A large friction-driven U.N.C.L.E. car was produced in South America, most probably in Argentina, by the firm Carlos V. It appears that the firm produced several different models in a variety of different colours. The boxes for them all appear to be the same, showing a crude rendition of the artwork from the Corgi Toys die-cast model.

Chapter Seven
Milton Bradley Products and Jigsaws

America's largest board game company, Milton Bradley, may have lost the U.N.C.L.E. game contract to Ideal Toys, but the company was successful in securing a licence to produce a pair of card games and several jigsaw puzzles. Among Milton Bradley's first products was The Man from U.N.C.L.E. Card Game in 1965. Priced at $1.39, this simple card game came in an illustrated box containing cards, counters and a small tray. The card backs were illustrated with an image of Napoleon. This same card game was sublicensed and produced by the firm Jumbo in Germany the following year.

The Man from U.N.C.L.E. Card Game was successful enough that in 1966 Milton Bradley would produce another card game. Strictly speaking it was effectively the same game (both being a variation of the card game rummy) but this time repackaged and branded as the Illya Kuryakin Card Game. The cards featured Illya's image on the reverse instead of Napoleon's. Once again this was priced at $1.39.

The only other game issued by Milton Bradley was the Shoot Out Game, which was also produced in 1965. This was a fairly simple marble game for two players. Marbles were flicked towards targets on the middle of a moulded playing base and players had to knock

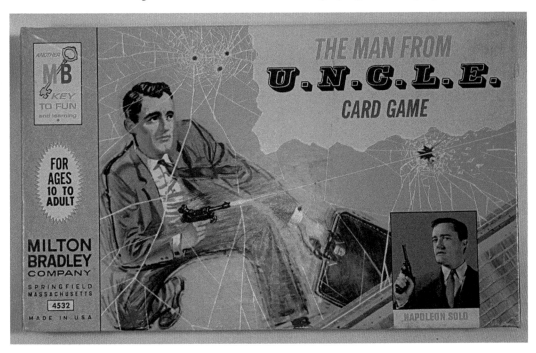

Card game.

Above: Card game contents.

Left: German card game.

Illya card game.

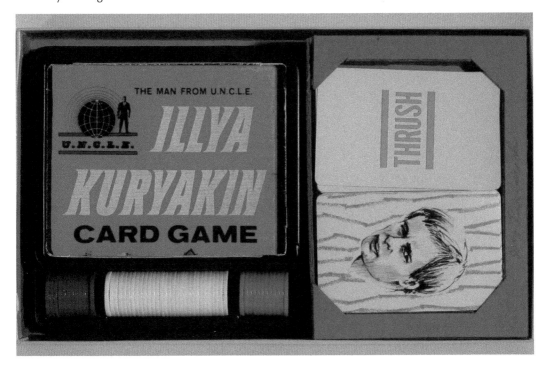

Illya card game contents.

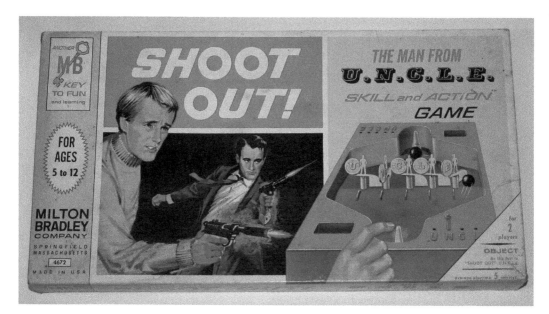

Shoot Out game box.

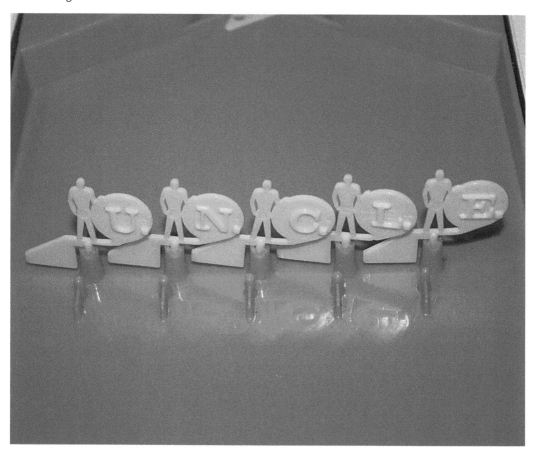

Shoot Out game contents.

five small figures all standing next to a letter spelling out 'U.N.C.L.E.'. The winner was the first player who managed to spell the word 'U.N.C.L.E.' by flipping the targets.

Milton Bradley was also the producer of two jigsaw puzzles for the series. The first series of puzzles was a set of four mystery puzzles produced in 1965. This featured a new idea at the time. Only a proportion of the puzzle's picture was shown on the box lid and each puzzle contained a booklet with a short mystery story. The solution to the mystery story was found upon completion of the jigsaw. These jigsaws each contained 600 pieces and sold for an original price of 79¢ each. The set of four puzzles were named as following: The Impossible Escape, The Micro Film Affair, The Loyal Groom, and The Vital Observation.

With the continued success of the series, and in particular the increased popularity of Illya, in 1966 Milton Bradley produced a second series of jigsaws, this time in their junior range, called the Illya Kuryakin Puzzles. There were only two puzzles in this second range which saw Illya featured prominently in the images. The titles in this series were Illya Crushes THRUSH and Illya's Battle Below. These two 100-piece puzzles were originally priced at 49¢ each.

The Impossible Escape.

The Micro Film Affair.

The Loyal Groom.

The Vital Observation.

Illya Crushes THRUSH.

Illya's Battle Below.

UK jigsaw The Getaway.

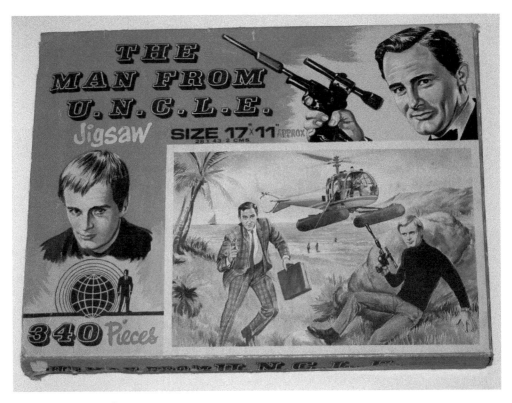

UK jigsaw Secret Plans.

UK jigsaw Solo in Trouble.

UK jigsaw The Frogman Affair.

Box back showing the four designs.

Two other firms also produced jigsaws. In the UK a firm called Thomas Hope & Sankey Hudson Ltd produced a series of four puzzles in 1966. Though he is not credited on the puzzles themselves, they featured artwork by the now-renowned comic artist Walt Howarth. Mr Howarth was responsible for artwork on many of the popular TV-related World Distributors annuals produced in the UK. All four puzzles, which were produced exclusively for Woolworths in the UK, are around 17 inches by 11 inches in size when completed, containing approximately 340 pieces, and sold for around 2s 9d. The designs in this set were titled The Getaway, Secret Plans, Solo in Trouble, and The Frogman Affair.

The final jigsaw puzzles produced were a set of three frame tray puzzles, which were produced by Jaymar Specialities in 1965. These were only sold as a set of three, coming packaged together in a cardboard sleeve. Each of these is approximately 14 inches by 11 inches in size and the three designs are not titled. The first one depicts Mr Waverley looking at a viewing screen image of Napoleon and Illya on a large computer. The second shows Napoleon rescuing Illya from two Arabs who have him chained in a cell. And the final puzzle of the set shows both Napoleon and Illya swimming under water with an unnamed woman, possibly intended to be April Dancer.

Earlier in this book, the U.N.C.L.E. Invisible Writing Cartridge Pen by Platignum was mentioned, but this was not the only U.N.C.L.E. pen to be produced. In 1966, a US firm called American Character produced what it called a Secret Message Pen for the show.

Jaymar frame puzzle 1.

Jaymar frame puzzle 2.

Jaymar frame puzzle 3.